Like Mother Like Daughter

Like Mother Like Daughter

David Baird

MQP

PUBLISHED BY MQ PUBLICATIONS LIMITED
12 THE IVORIES, 6–8 NORTHAMPTON STREET
LONDON N1 2HY
TEL: +44 (0) 20 7359 2244
FAX: +44 (0) 20 7359 1616

EMAIL: MAIL@MQPUBLICATIONS.COM
WEBSITE: WWW.MQPUBLICATIONS.COM

COPYRIGHT © 2004 MQ PUBLICATIONS LIMITED
TEXT COMPILATION © 2004 DAVID BAIRD
ARTWORK © 2004 JANET BOLTON

ISBN: 1-84072-612-1

10 9 8 7 6 5 4 3 2 1

PRINTED AND BOUND IN CHINA

If my daughter, Liza, wants to become an actress, I'll do everything to help her.

JUDY GARLAND

You teach your daughters the diameters of the planets and wonder when you are done that they do not delight in your company.

SAMUEL JOHNSON

Art is the child of Nature; yes, her darling child, in whom we trace the features of the mother's face, her aspect, and her attitude.

HENRY WADSWORTH LONGFELLOW

To describe my mother would be to write about a hurricane in its perfect power.

MAYA ANGELOU

Youth fades; love droops,
the leaves of friendship fall;
A mother's secret hope
outlives them all.

OLIVER WENDELL HOLMES, SR.

15

Oh my son's my son till he gets him a wife, but my daughter's my daughter all her life.

DINAH MULOCK CRAIK

The older I get the more of my mother I see in myself.

NANCY FRIDAY

He that would the daughter win must with the mother first begin.

ENGLISH PROVERB

The bearing and the training of a child Is woman's wisdom.

ALFRED, LORD TENNYSON

"Do you know who made you?"
"Nobody, as I knows on," said
the child, with a short laugh.
The idea appeared to amuse
her considerably; for her eyes
twinkled, and she added,
"I 'spect I growed. Don't think
nobody never made me."

HARRIET ELIZABETH BEECHER STOWE

A mother's arms are made of tenderness and children sleep soundly in them.

Victor Hugo

Ought not education to bring out and fortify the differences rather than the similarities? For we have too much likeness as it is....

VIRGINIA WOOLF

There came to port last Sunday night
The queerest little craft,
Without an inch of rigging on;
I looked and looked—and laughed.
It seemed so curious that she
Should cross the unknown water,
And moor herself within my room—
My daughter! O, my daughter!

GEORGE WASHINGTON CABLE

I carry from my mother's womb a fanatic's heart.

WILLIAM BUTLER YEATS

A mother's happiness is like a beacon, lighting up the future but reflected also on the past in the guise of fond memories.

HONORÉ DE BALZAC

Then, my good girls, be
    more than women, wise:
At least be more than I
    was; and be sure
You credit anything the
    light gives life to
Before a man.

FRANCIS BEAUMONT AND JOHN FLETCHER

How the mother is to be pitied who hath handsome daughters! Locks, bolts, bars, and lectures of morality are nothing to them: they break through them all. They have as much pleasure in cheating a father and mother, as in cheating at cards.

John Gay

Do not be dismayed daughters, at the
number of things which you have to
consider before setting out on this divine
journey, which is the royal road to heaven.
By taking this road we gain such precious

treasures that it is no wonder if the cost
seems to us a high one. The time will come
when we shall realize that all we have paid
has been nothing at all by comparison with
the greatness of our prizes.

St. Teresa of Avila

The tie which links mother and child is of such pure and immaculate strength as to be never violated.

WASHINGTON IRVING

Sweet babe, in thy face
Soft desires I can trace,
Secret joys and secret smiles,
Little pretty infant wiles.

William Blake

Oh, high is the price of parenthood, and daughters may cost you double. You dare not forget, as you thought you could, that youth is a plague and a trouble.

Phyllis McGinley

I think, at a child's birth, if a mother could ask a fairy godmother to endow it with the most useful gift, that gift would be curiosity.

ELEANOR ROOSEVELT

All women become like their mothers. That is their tragedy. No man does. That is his.

Oscar Wilde

A mother is the truest friend we have, when trials heavy and sudden, fall upon us; when adversity takes the place of prosperity; when friends who rejoice with us in our sunshine desert us; when trouble thickens around us, still will she cling to us, and endeavor by her kind precepts and counsels to dissipate the clouds of darkness, and cause peace to return to our hearts.

WASHINGTON IRVING

Women are told from their infancy, and taught by the example of their mothers, that a little knowledge of human weakness, justly termed cunning, softness of temper, outward obedience, and a scrupulous attention to a puerile kind of propriety, will obtain for them the protection of man.

MARY WOLLSTONECRAFT

Don't be discouraged if your children reject your advice. Years later they will offer it to their own offspring.

ANONYMOUS

Who ran to help me
   when I fell,
And would some pretty
   story tell,
Or kiss the place to
   make it well?
My mother.

ANN TAYLOR

A daughter is a mother's gender partner, her closest ally in the family confederacy, an extension of her self. And mothers are their daughters' role model, their biological and emotional road map, the arbiter of all their relationships.

Victoria Secunda

The best academy, a mother's knee.

JAMES RUSSELL LOWELL

Sweet smile, the
daughter of the
Queen of love,
Expressing all thy
mother's powerful art.

EDMUND SPENSER

Whatever else is unsure in this stinking dunghill of a world a mother's love is not.

JAMES JOYCE

Thou art thy mother's glass, and she in thee
Calls back the lovely April of her prime.

WILLIAM SHAKESPEARE

No one in the world can take the place of your mother. Right or wrong, from her viewpoint you are always right. She may scold you for little things, but never for the big ones.

HARRY TRUMAN

The future destiny of the child is always the work of the mother.

NAPOLEON BONAPARTE

73

Education commences at the mother's knee, and every word spoken within hearsay of little children tends toward the formation of character.

HOSEA BALLOU

As long as a woman can look ten years younger than her own daughter, she is perfectly satisfied.

My mother had a slender, small body, but a large heart—a heart so large that everybody's joys found welcome in it, and hospitable accommodation.

MARK TWAIN

What do girls do who haven't any mothers to help them through their troubles?

Louisa May Alcott

There was a place
  in childhood that
  I remember well,
And there a voice
  of sweetest tone
  bright fairy tales
  did tell.

SAMUEL LOVER

Admiration; is our polite recognition of another's resemblance to ourselves.

AMBROSE BIERCE

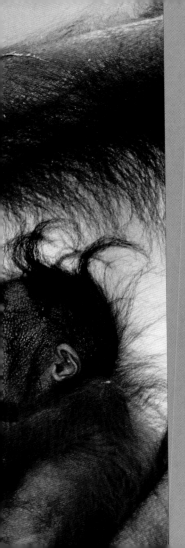

Every dung beetle is a gazelle in the eyes of its mother.

MOORISH PROVERB

My mother drew a distinction between achievement and success. She said that achievement is the knowledge that you have studied and worked hard and done the best that is in you. Success is being praised by others. That is nice but not as important or satisfying. Always aim for achievement and forget about success.

HELEN HAYES

Love the whole world as a mother loves her only child.

BUDDHA

The desolation and terror of, for the first time, realizing that the mother can lose you, or you her, and your own abysmal loneliness and helplessness without her.

FRANCIS THOMPSON

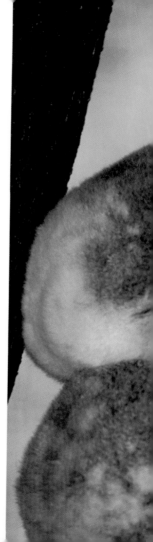

If you must hold yourself up to your children as an object lesson, hold yourself up as a warning and not an example.

GEORGE BERNARD SHAW

Photo Credits

Text Credits